is
there
love
here?

yasmin jasmy

Copyright © 2023 Yasmin Jasmy

Published by Yasmin Jasmy
Petaling Jaya, Selangor
mind-pause.com

ISBN 978-629-98073-0-8 (Print) 978-629-98073-1-5 (Digital)

Cataloguing-in-Publication Data
A catalogue record for this book is available
from the National Library of Malaysia.

Cover design by Benard Uwuondo
Illustrations by Benard Uwuondo
Typesetting by Teaspoon Publishing

for little amin

WORDS

words nurture –
they propel us as quickly
as they burn us –
it's how we use them.

words reshape our
lives; they shed light
on our shadows; they
amplify.

words make us
real – they
describe the experiences
we feel and they create a world in
which our pain
exists.

THE LAMP

reflection is the lamp
of
the heart

START HERE

I

There is
power
in sharing the heart's questions,
and the answers
when we find
them.

II

"Love is the will to extend [oneself] for the purpose of nurturing one's own or another's spiritual growth." A definition Bell Hooks borrowed from M. Scott Peck's book *The Road Less Travelled*. Lying on the grass, reading these words for the first time, I cried. The words 'spiritual growth' felt right in my heart.

Upon reading that definition so many questions burst out in my mind. What if we experience spiritual decay, then? Is that an absence of love? Are we aware of the actions that cause spiritual decay in our relationships to ourselves and others? For the purposes of this book, I call the actions or inactions that give rise to pain and suffering "not-love".

Interestingly, people with a history of abuse or neglect are more likely to suffer from depression, substance abuse, and other behavioural issues than those who do not.[1,2] This aligns with the idea that not-love leads to forms of spiritual decay. We also cannot ignore how our physical health is influenced by our spiritual health, as is seen in heart patients.[3]

Our intelligent bodies have been signalling, calling us to pay attention to the status of the heart – is it benefitting or suffering from the quality of our closest relationships and regular interactions? Unfortunately for us and contrary to dominant belief, **love is not blind** – it sees with eyes and ears wide open, absorbing everything it encounters. Thus, it is time to take stock of our experience and ask ourselves: Is there love here?

III

I organised this book into two parts: Not-love & Love. Not-love deals with what hurts a heart and Love with what pleases it.
This is how
it'll make sense to the mind,
but the way it'll make sense to the heart
is by reading between the
lines.

---

[1] The Relation Between Child Maltreatment and Adolescent Suicidal Behavior: A Systematic Review and Critical Examination of the Literature (Miller, Esposito-Smythers, Weismoore, Renshaw 2013)

[2] Adverse Childhood Experiences and Early Maladaptive Schemas in Adulthood: A Systematic Review and Meta-Analysis (Pilkington, Bishop, Younan 2020)

[3] Meta-Analysis of Anxiety as a Risk Factor for Cardiovascular Disease (Emdin, Odutayo, Wong, Tran, Hsiao, Hunn 2016)

PART 1: NOT-LOVE

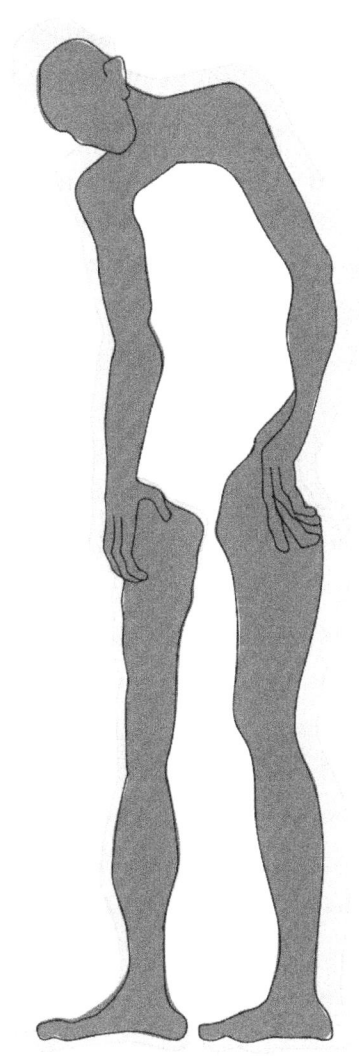

1: SELF-NEGLECT

Love nurtures us to the point of expansion. When we don't grow or struggle to self-actualise, there is a need to ask: have I been neglecting myself? Concrete examples of the things that *do not* nurture and affect our growth are having a negative sense of self or staying in environments that are abusive or neglectful.

2: TO ENGAGE IN PAINFUL RITUALS

Am I being offered neglect, abuse, or manipulation in the form of love? Us humans engage in painful rituals that are designed to break us. We re-produce or re-enact cultures in our homes, schools, communities, and politics that are anti-growth, and we wonder why we are suffering.

3: TO IGNORE THE WISDOM OF OUR BODIES

We say emotional pain is invisible – but we would see it if we truly opened our eyes. We'd see it in the way we drag our feet; in the way we live on autopilot; in the way we numb ourselves; in the way our bodies forget how to breathe.

Imagine if our ancestors did not run away from the lions they saw? They would get eaten and we would not be here if they stayed put and told themselves it was all in the mind. We might not encounter lions in our daily lives today, but we still face dangers that our bodies have every reason to alert us to. Our bodies protect us by making sure we stay away from things that might hinder our survival. It hurts us to ignore these signs of malaise.

4:   TO LIVE INAUTHENTICALLY

Maybe you are not allowing your heart to shine through because you've been told who you are is not enough. Maybe your genuine feelings have been punished or neglected so you learn to hide them. Not expressing our authentic selves leads to spiritual decay as we become a shell of ourselves.

When we perform to keep their attention, afraid of losing their affections and acceptance, we become a stranger to ourselves. This jarring internal disconnect we feel breaks our hearts and limits our expansion.

ALONE WITH OUR DEMONS

we do not deserve to
be in the dark,
alone with our demons.

I HAVE WRONGED ME

i am
not angry
because you have wronged me.
i am angry because
i
have wronged
me,
by ignoring what my
heart wants and what
my soul
needs.

ALREADY THE CONSTELLATION

my worth clung
on to your approval;
blinded to who
i really was,
my blindness held me
underwater

gasping for air
i
fought to see the sun in me;
i
fought to believe that i
never needed
your stars –
i was already
the constellation

WITHIN

i brought myself
to ruin. i believed an
illusion
that love & peace could not,
did not
exist
within

BEGGING FOR SCRAPS

you beg them for scraps,
forgetting that you are rich
in what you are asking for.

SHIT INTO GOLD

i tortured my soul
trying to turn
shit into
gold

NO MIND GYMNASTICS

the kind of relationship i'm available for:
- i see evidence of love and respect
- i never have to play guessing games
- i see evidence of being a priority

the kind of relationship i'm not available for:
- i don't see evidence of love and respect
- i do mind gymnastics
- i have to prove myself or become someone else to deserve their time and affections

I DON'T BUY IT

i don't want it, i don't buy it –
the idea
that i am not
enough
as i
am

NEVER TRIES TO LEAVE

i don't have to grasp for what
is truly mine.

what is truly mine never
tries to leave.

THE HARSHEST OPPRESSOR

oppressors on the news aren't the harshest
ones i know.

the cruellest oppressor i know never lets me
rest;
criticises me despite my
best, despite
all the ways
i've grown.

DOORS

love can't get through if
the doors to
your
heart
are
heavy

I KNOW WHAT IT TASTES LIKE

i am careful of what i consume. i recognise the taste
of
venom from a heart that knows not of consideration.
i know what it tastes like –

the bitterness of unhealed pain.

I REMEMBER

you don't remember
your careless strike to my
heart but i
remember. i pay for it with
my
peace.

GENERATIONAL TRAUMA:

a cycle that is
hard to break
but that continues to
break
us

SHATTERED HEARTS

my shattered heart
made me believe
i was not good enough,
pretty enough,
smart enough
for love

our shattered hearts
made us believe
we weren't good enough,
pretty enough,
smart enough
to love
each other

A NOTE ABOUT LOVE

love doesn't erase my needs,
obliterate my voice,
or put me last.

A SLAVE TO DYSFUNCTION (ENMESHMENT)

i cannot survive without your
gaze.

i cannot survive without your
grip.

i am lost without your
emotions –
i embrace them as my
own.

a slave to dysfunction,
all i've ever known.

SURVIVAL

my body survived you
but my heart
did not.

NO STRENGTH FOR MY DREAMS

so broken
from
my nightmares,
i
have no strength
for
my dreams

WE ALL OWN ONE

he broke my heart
like he didn't own one
himself

IF WE TOOK OUR VOWS TO GOD MORE SERIOUSLY

two gifts from God that truly test us: our
spouse and our
children. gifts so precious, we perform
ceremonies to welcome them.
i don't know about you,
but sometimes i wish life came with a
how-to-appreciate-your-gifts-from-God
manual. but i have a feeling we
wouldn't need one
if
we took our vows to God
more
seriously.

IT'S NOT-LOVE

when they
cause
insecurity in your mind,
chaos in your soul, and
dis-ease
in your body,
it's not love.

NOT-LOVE PT. II

since we cannot agree on what
love is
maybe it's good enough
for now
to agree on what love is
not:

control
manipulation
abuse
disrespect
exploitation

how is real love
different from everything
we've known?

YOU SAY YOU LOVE ME BUT

you say you love me
but
we are lost in
translation

you say you love me
but
i don't see
your actions

you say you love me
but
i don't
feel it

you say you love me
but
i
don't
believe it

A LANGUAGE SO UGLY

what's your
anti-love
language?
something that
does not speak to your heart at all –
a language so ugly
it taints the people
who speak it.

LOVING OTHERS

it is simple:
if you want to
love them, learn what makes
them feel
neglected,

and never commit it.

NO SENSE AT ALL

born to share our hearts and gifts
but the world
scared us into hiding.

born to love but
the world scarred us into
hating.

it makes both complete sense
and no sense
at all.

YOUR FACE

i see your face
every time i get asked
what burned my
soul long enough
to ignite

ON TRAUMA

no one talks about
the flashbacks you get
when you've been manipulated
you will see a liar in
everyone
you
meet

THE CRIME OUR TONGUES COMMIT

we are terrified of being vulnerable,
of how exposed we'd feel
if we were touched or seen by
another.

we say we prefer isolation,
but that is a crime our tongues commit. worst of all,
we pretend – we act
like it doesn't kill us
not to
love.

DEPTHS OF US

curious about deep seas
but
unfascinated by what
lies beneath our surface. uninterested in
the depths
of
us.

THEY SAY MENTAL HEALTH IS INVISIBLE

they say mental health is invisible but
i see it
in the way i am
uninterested
in what i used to love;
in the way my
body
does everything i
don't want it to; in the way
my
body won't
sleep; in the way
i let these substances
numb me

LISTEN

we change ourselves to relieve
our depression
we blame ourselves to turn around
our misfortune

but sometimes it helps to ask a tough question – is
it depression or is it
that people around
us
don't listen?

WE LET OURSELVES BLEED

we soothe crying babies like
it's the death of
us
but we let ourselves
bleed till
the death of us

GOD'S HEART

i see so much wrong in the world that i wonder
if
God's heart
is breaking
a friend once said to me during a moment of misery
if your misery makes me feel compassion imagine
how God must be
feeling

REDHA

it's in the small acts of giving our pain the permission
to exist, it's in the *redha* or acceptance of what our
souls carry, that we may feel free.

ANXIETY

anxiety is:
a constricted chest
a pulsating heart
a warm body
a racing mind
needs unmet

NOT JUST IN THE MIND

mental health is not just
in
the mind, it is
felt
all through
the body

OUR BODIES WILL SPEAK

how it *feels* is more important than how it *looks*. it
doesn't matter how well we dress
our pain up. our bodies
know when we are acting, performing, and
pretending to be okay.
our bodies will speak when our mouths haven't
found the words to say.

PANIC ATTACK

it has felt like death since my
first panic attack
constantly on edge to
keep from going over the edge

JOY & CHAOS

concern yourself with
your joys
but have knowledge
of
the things that
disrupt your spirit

AN UNWRITTEN LAW

i follow an unwritten law
that steals my joy
and breaks me down

a few weeks of rest
is not a reward;
it is
an
incentive

i am shackled
to a system designed with
not-me
in mind

WHAT IF

we look away from crimes committed
onto others – but
what if
God
looks away
when we need His
justice?

WHERE CAN I BUY SOME?

running out of

~~coffee~~

~~eggs~~

~~milk~~

coping mechanisms

A PRAYER & A DESPERATE WISH:

may i please You
for i could not live
without
some heaven to look forward
to

THE MOULD

to fit into the mould
you created,
i'll first have to
break

MY SOUL DISAGREES

my soul disagrees
with the pace we live in

i am not a robot
but i am treated like a machine

NEVER CONTENT

your spirit was perfected
but you let their words burn
into your skin
and turn you into
ashes you did not
recognise.

THICK SKIN

your words feel like sticks
and stones on my skin.

you poke me until
i give in.

i did not have
thick skin, but you helped
me with that.

i hope you use your
words to heal
instead.

A SOLID FOUNDATION

to
endure rough
weather, we build strong
homes. but we do not build
our relationships with that much thought.

YOUR POISON

i was consuming
your poison as part of my
daily diet, and i
did not realise
it

LONELINESS

eating on your own is not
sad
or lonely – like being
in their company

EACH TIME

each time i please you
that's a choice i make

each time i forgive you
that's a choice i make

each time i love you
that's a choice i make

each time you prove me wrong
that's a choice you make

ON GRATITUDE

gratitude is medicinal but we prescribe gratitude like
we buy fast fashion – have some and you'll be good
'til the next season of depression. we assume that
those who are suffering are ungrateful but gratitude is
like a balm – it soothes our wounds but if our
wounds are deep, we'll need a fucking village to fix it.

SO WHY DO YOU?

God doesn't stop being God
because people
disagree with
or dislike Him

God doesn't stop being God
when people hate,
abandon,
or reject Him

A CARICATURE

a disgrace –
to turn oneself
into someone else's idea of
perfection

a disaster –
shape-shifting our souls
to satisfy their
illusions

a disease –
when we make
a caricature of ourselves
for their entertainment

IT SHOWS

we hide how we really feel
and it
shows

SAFE

the world doesn't
feel safe
to me,
i respond to
it differently.
i am not broken!
i don't need to be
saved!
i need to feel
safe

IS IT TOO MUCH TO ASK

this body feels strange to me,
is it too much to
ask
to want the body you live in
to feel like
home?

ALL I NEEDED

when i needed warmth, what i needed was you
when i needed safety, what i needed was you
when i needed protection, what i needed was you
all i needed was you

99 PROBLEMS & MY BRAIN CREATES THEM ALL

my brain will always be good at
finding problems in the present

when one problem resolves
another begins
i can't win

i can't trust my brain to feel peace
these are the cards i've been dealt

WHEN YOU REFUSED TO BE HELD ONTO

we tell ourselves
beautiful stories
to soothe the part of us
that needs to hear them, not realising
that what it needs to hear
is the truth

i focused on the little
gestures i saw you
make, because all i had were your
gestures
and not you

i needed you so much that
i created a relationship in
my mind – it may
or may not
have been fiction but
it was a story i held onto
when you refused to be held onto

OVERGIVER

oh! overgiver,
they call you all kinds of names,
people pleaser,
caretaker

oh! overgiver,
you are a river
with an endless supply
of love
from the Source
of love

undergivers are the real perpetrators

DEATH OF ME

i've grieved the death of loved ones before –
absolutely – but grieving us
was the death of
me

THINKING OUT LOUD

i find that anger usually
stems from a clash of values
we spend days, months,
even years
in anger because of clashing principles
we blame ourselves for being unforgiving – others
blame us for not being over it.

how can we compromise
and co-exist? i asked
whose priorities are more important – yours
or mine?
maybe you are afraid of my truth
maybe i am afraid of you
maybe we are just damned fools.

YEARNING

the only thing constant about you was your
absence
i wonder if i ever loved you or just
yearned for you
(there's a difference)

CHAINS

you've already lost me
my eyes, my ears
you've already lost me
i've broken your chains
you've already lost me
i've outgrown your ways
i've outgrown the version of me who
needed
you

it is simple
if they love you, you'll know
but is it really that simple to know if anyone
loves you
at all?
i've spent my days digging for answers – who loves
me,
who doesn't?
my lists are long, my patience thin
these guys never really loved me –
these ones did!
if they really loved you
it's not that you'd know. it's that they'd know and
people who know will show

SELF-LOVE, CHECK

loving others comes
naturally, loving myself
takes practice
loving others is
easier than loving the
person i'm always
with

loving myself feels
like a chore, one more thing on
my to-do list
i wish it were different
i wish it were easier than this

I'M SORRY

i'm sorry for who i
was when we met
what i know now i
hadn't yet
i'm sorry i broke your trust and that
i was immature
i'm sorry it took some time for me to
know love

NOT GOOD ENOUGH

i've never been able
to let somebody in since
you

if the space you once occupied
wasn't good enough for you
then who would it
be good enough
to?

ON TRAUMA PT. II

when i recovered from the worst i thought
the worst
was over but i lived
expecting
the other shoe to fall
expecting my reality to break
when i recovered from the worst i thought
the worst
was over but nobody talks about how
it's hard to remember yourself when
you only remember the shock
haunted by what-ifs like what
if it happens again and this time i don't
win?
when i recovered from the worst i thought
the worst
was over and *it was* –
thank God

SOPHISTICATED

the emotional weights i carried got pretty heavy over
time and i wish i was trained on how to understand
the language of my heart.
i would express my feelings carelessly or suppress
them just as carelessly which buried my feelings even
deeper into my psyche.
this became unhealthy.
i thought i was invincible but it turns out i was (still
am) susceptible to the crushing weight of my
emotions and some days i'd tear my hair out because
nothing made sense but the heart is not difficult –
she is simply sophisticated.
not everyone understands advanced math equations.
it takes – a lot of – patience, willingness, and some
talent.
it takes someone special to recognise the love that is
(not) here.

IT'S NOT A CRIME TO BE YOURSELF

i pretend to be happy, like nothing bothers me,
showing you a face i think you'll approve of. i
pretend to be happy, like nothing bothers me,
desiring to connect, to be loved, and to belong. but
things bother me
and i get sad sometimes
why do i think being myself is a
crime?
i have questions in my mind that i
feel too shy to ask; i have ideas that are
too weird to discuss
love me for my quirks for my heart and
my mind
love me even when i say i'm not fine

.

HARDSHIPS ARE MEANT TO BE HARD

hardships are meant to be hard but we
make light of them
we pretend we have it easy we pretend we are
free of our chains and pain we pretend we're not
weighed down
i can handle this myself but i
don't want to
i need your help i want to
hear words of relief i want peace just like you
do

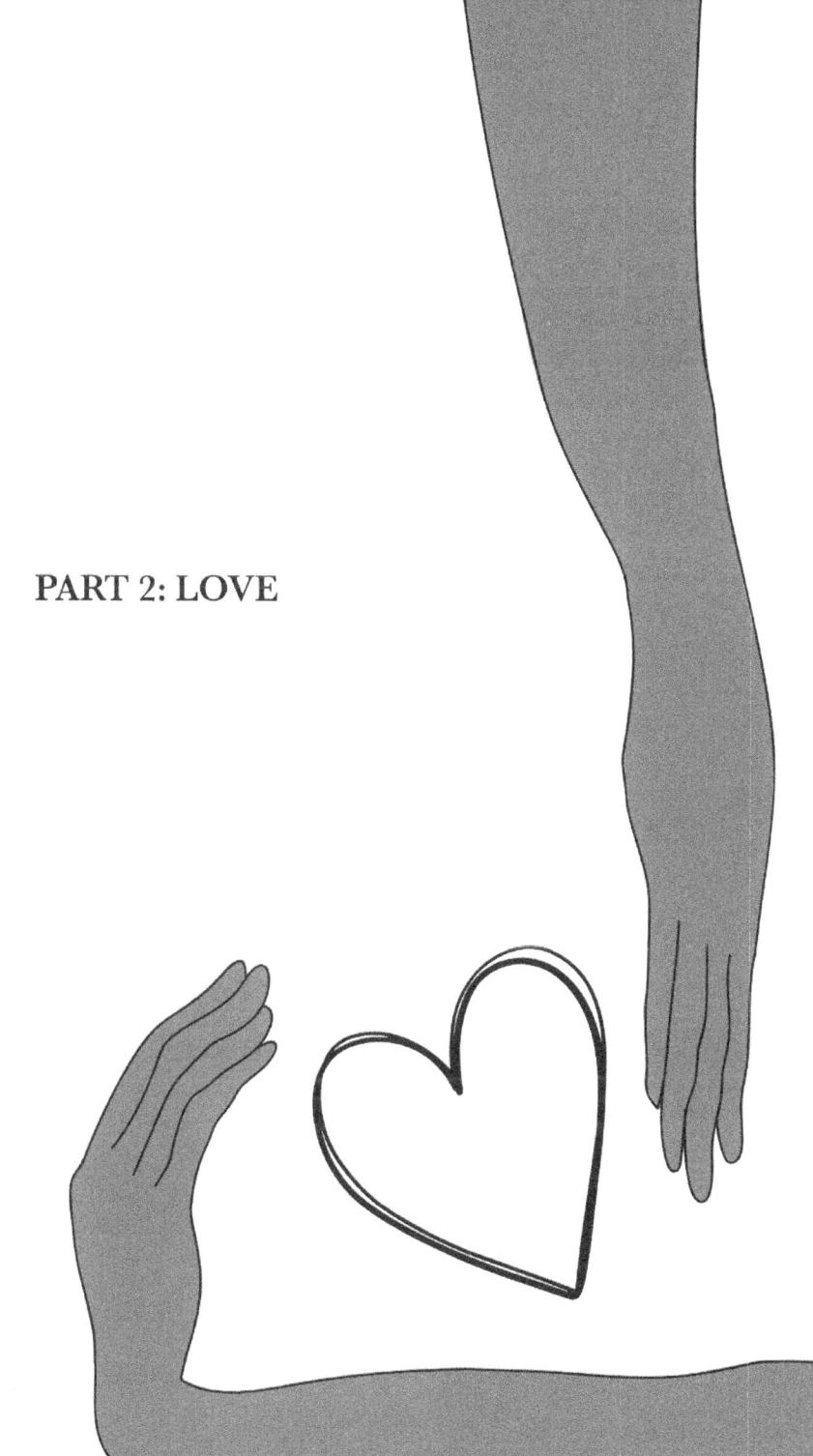

PART 2: LOVE

1:   TO HELP OURSELVES WHEN WE NEED IT

Have the willpower to make changes when you see yourself diminishing. Waking up every day to what feels like a nightmare and not doing anything about it is neglectful - and we have said self-neglect is not-love. I once read *Hell Yeah or No* by Derek Sivers where he says, "everything is my fault ... now you're the person who made things happen, made a mistake, and can learn from it." If it is my fault I don't like my life, then it is within my power to take the necessary steps to make changes.

We do not have to address our shortcomings or mistakes in a cruel way. We can do it with deep compassion - through embodying these concepts by Dr. Kristin Neff:

- *Self-kindness* vs self-judgement

- *Common humanity* vs isolation

- *Mindfulness* vs over-identification

The second component - our common humanity - particularly stood out to me, as we often feel alone in our individual experiences. Our 'common humanity' serves as a reminder that we are not the first nor will we be the last to experience what we are experiencing

– whether it be a job loss or change, struggles at university, a divorce.

*

The practices that helped me were mindfulness, writing, movement, and using my imagination.

First, in a lecture by Jon Kabat-Zinn, founder of the Mindfulness-Based Stress Reduction Program, he explains that the essence of **mindfulness** is the presence of the heart. The Chinese character for mindfulness (念), where he derived this from, tells us that the heart is present in any mindfulness practice. With the heart present, we have the opportunity to get to know her, listen to her, and pay attention to how she feels.

Imagine being in a forest so silent you can hear the rustling of leaves. This is what it means to be mindful – it is being open to our soul's whispers. While we connect to its wisdom, we obtain solutions to create more balance and harmony both within and around us.

Writing is an extension of my mindfulness practice where I have the space to express my feelings in a safe container – my journal. Experimental research by James Pennebaker suggests that *writing* benefits us by helping us with the stories and emotions that we store in our bodies. A particular brand of writing, *reflective writing*, has helped me relieve my daily stresses. Writing poems helps me express myself by lending me the structure to express myself in just a few words – a few words is better than nothing.

Our bodies are intelligent, and they are a bottomless resource of goodness. *Movement* or moving our bodies is a great way to access that resource – especially when we feel down or stuck. It is another mindful practice I acquired. I dance when I want to feel free and happy. Putting on a good song and dancing to it first thing in the morning has not let me down yet. It is a great way to boost my energy.

Lastly, *using our imagination* is powerful and easy. Scientists have shown that our minds believe anything we tell them. By imagining good, expansive, and happy thoughts, our minds believe they are happening in the present moment. This triggers a release of hormones in our systems that correspond to those thoughts. There is no limit to our imagination, so we might as well use it to uplift ourselves. We can do this through writing or by simply closing our eyes and letting our minds do their magic. Imagine living your happiest, most expansive life. And do it often.

2:   TO PAY ATTENTION TO WHAT DOES NOT FEEL RIGHT

One of the most nurturing acts is self-validation. Validate yourself, your hurts, and your experience of what is going on. Do not wait for someone to confirm it – your heart already knows the truth. We live in a fast-paced culture that also denies the wisdom of our body, so we may not naturally listen to what it is saying. By listening to its subtle messages, we address what holds us back and create space for what can propel us.

3: TO BUILD A NETWORK OF LOVE IN YOUR LIFE

I have interacted with many individuals over the course of my young adult life through studies and travels. From my observations, the ones that seemed to be flourishing in their respective fields had a strong network of love established in their lives – which I define as a network of supportive and nurturing relationships with ourselves and the humans, projects, and hobbies we care about.

This solid foundation becomes the source of our personal strength as we leap into a world full of unknowns. It becomes a reference point when we feel unsure about ourselves and others. It becomes a form of protection as we engage with strangers.

When our lives are a work of art, we will be more careful about who paints on it.

4:   TO RADICALLY LOVE YOURSELF

Henry Ford once said: whether you think you can or whether you think you can't, you're right. Whether you believe you are inconsequential or wonderful – you are right. But the belief that will nurture your growth is one that is self-nourishing. See your inherent value and attribute amazing qualities to yourself. Remember your strengths and use them to propel yourself forward.

One Harvard scientist calculated and found that the probability of being born is close to zero.[1] I then flirted with the idea that if indeed it was almost impossible for me to exist, then wouldn't it be probable that I was *pre-destined* to exist? Which means that my existence was *not* an accident! This is an expansive belief, in my opinion.

Radically loving ourselves also means seeing who we truly are without judgement – including the parts that are harder to love. Borrow Dr. Kristin Neff's self-compassion framework (refer to Love, 1: To Help Ourselves When We Need It) and be kind to yourself as you embrace your shortcomings. You are not the only one in the world with them. Neff also found that

---

[1] Dr. Ali Binazir wrote in a 2011 blogpost on Harvard.edu that he estimates the probability of being born as 1 in 10 to the power of 2,685,000. The blogsite has since been archived.

we are more likely to flourish when we address our shortcomings kindly rather than ignore them religiously.

5: TO NURTURE YOUR UNPLEASANT FEELINGS

Learning to nurture our feelings helps us expand because our feelings teach us what our values and boundaries are. Knowing our values and boundaries makes us stronger, more resilient, and self-sufficient.

Contrary to popular belief, unpleasant feelings are not inherently bad. Blocking ourselves from them limits our spiritual growth as we find ourselves without valuable information about our environment. Is this relationship right for me? Should I stay in this job? This is less about making permanent decisions than about making informed decisions. The information lies in how we feel about our individual situations.

Get curious about your feelings without judgement – befriend them with the aim of growth. We may find our feelings uncomfortable or unpleasant but there is purpose in what may seem like useless emotions that get in the way of our lives. Did you know that certain flowers bloom only in winter? Those flowers would not have the opportunity to bloom if we sped up or refused seemingly dire weather. Our sadness teaches us that something doesn't align with the heart. Our anger tells us something has crossed our boundaries or does not align with our values. Listen to how you feel and grow from what you hear.

6: TO NURTURE YOUR SHADOWS

Similar to accepting your feelings, learn to accept your shadows too. Your shadows are the parts of you that are seemingly negative. For example, we may refer to your tendency to be available for unavailable people as shadowy behaviour. We may even refer to your propensity for judging others as shadowy behaviour.

You know you're not doing yourself a favour by continuing these behaviours but they are aspects of you that have become so familiar. Accepting these behaviours or traits and learning from them is pro-growth because it creates space for a mature version of you to develop. When we do not understand our shadows, our shadows will continue impacting the relationship we have with ourselves and others.

Making peace with our shadows is a practice of humility too, as we come to terms with the nature of life – that we are here to make mistakes and learn from them.

7:   TO PICK THE WORDS YOU USE ON YOURSELF WITH CARE

I often talk about the sticky notes I post on my bathroom wall – the ones I started posting at the beginning of the pandemic – as an example of this. What started as a random desire to remember kind and uplifting phrases became a positive and affirming environment I could go back to at any time. This helped create a more positive and affirming environment within.

Your body tastes the flavour of your personal narrative. Sweet words help develop positive self-perception whereas bitterness helps destroy it. We need a healthy self-esteem to make something of ourselves – and this starts with surrounding ourselves with healthier and more optimistic inputs from our environment. Do the words and ideas we regularly consume inspire us? Do they lift us up?

8: TO NURTURE WHAT MAKES YOU HAPPY

You know that feeling you get when you eat your favourite meal? That same sense of delight and satisfaction exists for your hobbies, projects, and relationships. Pause your rational mind and dive into your heart – what gets you out of bed? Which relationships feel nurturing and expansive? Get curious about what lights you up – there is power in feeling excited about your life. Anything you look forward to is worth your time!

The joy your heart feels connecting to people and places that make you happy is the blueprint for your spiritual growth. It does not have to be a million different things either. One thing to be happy about is better than none.

9:   TO NURTURE YOUR INNER-CHILD

Our inner-child is the part of us that is tender – the heart of the heart, so to speak. Children are indeed needful, but their needs are basic: safety and nurturing care. An inner-child that feels unsafe and neglected may take over the driver's seat of our lives, which shows up as self-neglect and harming others. Many adults who experienced neglect during their formative years suffer from substance abuse.[5] Narcissism can also be explained by neglect or abuse experienced during our formative years.[6]

Learning to care for our inner-child sometimes feels like pushing a boulder up a hill, but the muscles you grow are worth it. It is through carefully and mindfully loving the child we were – that we are – that we can begin to experience ourselves (and others) more safely. A loved inner-child inspires us to see the world with fresh eyes and feel it with fresh skin.

---

[5] Child Maltreatment and Illicit Substance Abuse: A Systematic Review and Meta-Analysis of Longitudinal Studies (Halpern, Schuch, Scherer, Sordi, Pachado, Dalbosco, Fara, Penchasky, Kessler, Von Diemen 2018)
[6] Article: Narcissism as a Consequence of Trauma and Early Experiences by Dolores Mosquera and Anabel Gonzalez (European Society of Trauma and Dissociation website)

10: TO KNOW WITH CERTAINTY THAT YOU ARE LOVED

I was raised a Muslim but this is not a chapter about Islam. Rather it is about believing we are worthy of forgiveness and love – evident from the teachings of our respective faiths.

When my heart was in pieces, I found it excruciatingly difficult to forgive myself and to see myself in a good light. No matter what I did, I could not overcome deep guilt and shame. One serendipitous day, I found a book called *A World Without Islam* by Graham E. Fuller lying on my dining table. Although this book was not 'spiritual', I felt inspired to lean into my faith.

On my journey, I found uncountable examples and teachings in the Quran and Muhammad's (peace be upon him) life about forgiveness and love that helped expand my self-esteem.

It is just as important (if not more) to focus on God's compassion than His anger. We are free to connect to God's mercy over His punishment. Eradicate your self-loathing one reminder at a time, because if you are worthy of such boundless and unconditional love, you must not be all that bad.

11: TO LOVE CONSCIOUSLY

Peck writes that "[love] is an act of will – We do not have to love. We choose to love." To love consciously is to take accountability and responsibility for ourselves in relationship – both as the recipient and giver of love.

To love consciously means being empowered to act in a way that nurtures both yourself and the person you care about. Choosing to have tough conversations that inspire growth; choosing presence over neglect to inspire connection; choosing to set boundaries with them over abandoning yourself to inspire respect. There are many ways we can love more consciously, and it starts with believing we can and are worthy of it.

Sometimes the best choice is not very clear – but it is clear that doing what is best is connected to our self-awareness, our compassion, and our willingness to extend ourselves for the growth of someone else.

12: TO BE PRESENT IN THEIR PRESENCE

I learned how powerful presence was from my late grandfather, Ismail. I was very lucky that he had retired by the time I entered high school. Before school, I'd spend time reciting the Quran with him, and after school I'd spend the evening with him and my grandmother until my father would pick me up. We shared uncountable moments in between where we would engage in serious conversations or be silly. I felt seen and safe in his mature and secure presence.

Have you felt invisible in someone's presence before? You tell them something and their response was unrelated or indifferent? It may seem insignificant, but when we don't get emotional feedback from our surroundings – when we're ignored – it creates a dissonance within. Studies on attachment have further shown that infants suffer from absent-minded or unemphatic parenting.[7] Scientists label the condition of infants who have not received sensitive attention from their primary caregivers as disorganised, anxious, or avoidant. In essence, what they are saying is: we were built to be present with each other – or we suffer. If we did not need the presence of another

---

[7] Unresolved States of Mind, Anomalous Parental Behavior, and Disorganized Attachment: A Review and Meta-Analysis of a Transmission Gap (Madigan, Bakermans-Kranenburg, Van Ijzendoorn, Moran, Pederson, Benoit 2006)

human being, we would not have been born defenceless or needed nurturing in the womb of our mothers.

I owe my grandfather a great debt of gratitude for being present with me.

13: TO NURTURE THEIR SHADOWS

As humans, we will fall short of 'calm' or 'happy' on some days. It is not only okay, it is natural – calm and happy were not the only two feelings created for humans and life is filled with things to be worried about. To nurture our rich inner-world, we sometimes need rest, or space to safely express ourselves.

When we create some space in our relationships for our shadows to exist, we not only develop as an individual, we help our relationships. Making our relationships a safe and loving container for all of ourselves to exist nurtures us *on a soul level*. Nothing expands someone like being able to show up as a whole human being and still be loved.

Let me draw your attention to the relationship we have with our pets as there is wisdom to be gained there. I noticed that my late pet cat, Ice, still appreciated my presence even if my mood was low. That she patiently accompanied me as I cried about another disappointment, and that she found her place on my chest at night no matter how badly I did that day. This is what it is like to be loved as a whole person.

If it feels good in our hearts to have an animal companion whose loyalty and compassion do not falter depending on our emotional states, maybe there is reason to acquire that quality for our human relationships too.

14: TO APPRECIATE THAT WE HAVE DIFFERENT NEEDS TO GROW

Is it the fault of the rose if it does not grow in dry conditions – like a cactus would? An environment that is conducive to our growth does not have to look or feel like somebody else's. We would not blame the rose for not growing in the desert. It is okay if what we need to grow looks completely different from our peers'.

Our growth will look different too. I once read that some plants grow deep beneath ground, while some grow tall into the sky. If we don't stop any of them from growing, or force one to grow like the other, why do we do that to ourselves?

15: TO NURTURE WHAT MAKES US UNIQUE

No two leaves are alike, Mahatma Gandhi once said. Each of us are unique by design and there's brilliance and purpose in our differences. I once contemplated, wouldn't the sun lose its purpose if it tried to be the moon? Sometimes we do not understand the value of something until we polish it. We abandon, neglect, or discourage what makes us unique before that interest or skill gets to develop.

We might not value artists like we value accountants, but there is inherent value in both. We have different skills to apply and contribute to the evolution of the world. We get excited about different things and there is nothing inherently wrong with that.

When we are happily engaged in what we are doing, there is space for us to bloom. It is a lot more productive to create a nourishing environment for our unique brilliance to shine than to diminish it to fit certain paradigms.

SOMEONE YOU DON'T RECOGNISE

make it a point to love yourself
exactly the way
you need.

do the magic
of unlocking
the bottomless love
you have
inside you.

be the person
who nourishes you,
supports you,
accepts you.

then watch yourself grow
into someone
you don't recognise.

SELF-LOVE

when i wake up
i ask myself
what will make me feel
loved
today?
then i go do it.

WHY I WRITE #1

to honour my faculties.
my hand amplifies
what my heart feels
and perceives. it says
what my mouth won't
speak.

WHY I WRITE #5 & #8

#5

because the words in my body got too heavy
to carry.

#8

because my anger would have no place to go
otherwise.

ACT LIKE A CHILD

act
like a child!
imagine.
be curious.
cry.

play – even if you
feel it's a waste of time.
be an idiot.
be hysterical.
be ridiculous.
i'm
serious.

THE NECTAR

the sweetness of success
comes from the nectar
of perseverance

IMAGINE

my imagination
is my gift. it is essential that it functions
when nothing else
does.

THE ONE

i was the one who believed my cries;
the one who hugged me tight.
i was the one who drove me to the therapist;
the one who set my appointments.
i was the one who sat through hours of lessons on
personal development;
the one who made that investment.
i was the one who believed my grief;
the one who listened.
i was the one who made
the difference.

THE REASON

i am the reason i smile,
the reason i fly. and if
i fall,
i'll be the reason i rise.

DETOX

we absorb so much more
than we are
aware of;
more than we
need

i have a few go-to activities
for when my body needs a release
from the daily things
i carry

i talk, dance, write, move. in short, i express. what i
mean by express is 'to force out by pressure' by
merriam-webster.
although not commonly used in this context,
this definition works best.

i force out my stresses creatively, daily. i force out the
build-up of stuff in my body – an excretion of sorts. a
detox for my
personal
system.

THINGS WE DON'T ASK OURSELVES ENOUGH

#1
how do i feel about myself right now?

#23
how was my day, really?

IMAGINE PT. II

we ruminate our worries
our concerns
the past
the future
but we can teach
our minds
to have a little fun.

imagine the things
that bring us happiness,
what excites
us.

the point of imagination
is to bring us
some comfort
from the comfort
of our
bedrooms.

STILLNESS

a moment of pause,
in mindful stillness,
is the longest minute
we could ever experience.

KEEP GOING

a flower was first a seed;
the sun still rises
while everyone is
asleep

WHATEVER IT IS

set boundaries, have the confidence, learn the skill;
learn mindfulness, see a therapist, whatever it is –
feel and breathe again.

HEALING

healing is more than the courses we take. more than
the routines we create. healing is noticing the very
breath we are taking. it is in fully experiencing our
being. it is in believing that every step we take is a
stroke of brilliance in God's painting. it is taking in
the magic of everything we are seeing.

HIS WAND

an orchestra of emotions,
He conducts my life
with His wand. His name doesn't appear
on my phone, but i hear Him
just fine.

I HAVE STRAYED

the path before me
might be lonely
but the crowd
could not
offer me
solace

my peace
is in
accepting that
my hands
heart
and eyes
all have something to
say;
often it is that i
have strayed

YOU KNOW

~~parents know best~~
parents want the best for you –
but *you know* what's best
for
you

HEART

there is no heart
without hear, so listen
when your heart is
speaking.

MINDFUL LIVING

care about these things:
- your job
- your friends
- your address
- your routines
- your hobbies

PROCESS OF ELIMINATION

sometimes
it is less about what we need more of,
and more about
what
we *don't need*
anymore.

POUR LOVE INTO YOURSELF

pouring love unconditionally
into people or things that won't pour
back
will drain
you

i've learned that
having so much love and care to
give
is perfect but not when it's
perfectly
taken for granted

receive the benefits of your own
caring and loving nature by
pouring that care and love into
your projects, yourself, and
anything that improves your life – because
you of all people deserve to be loved
by you

THE OCEAN

it makes no difference to the ocean
when you pour
more water
into
it.

TO LOVE

to love is to
leap
with eyes and ears
wide
open. to see
safety
in their actions and hear honesty on
their
lips.

APPROVAL

suddenly i didn't feel
the need to seek anyone's
approval.
suddenly being myself
felt possible.

YOU

made of fire,
earth,
air,
water –
the perfect creation
that destroys
definitions.

YOU PT. II

a special blend of
sweet and bitter
notes;
a rich,
distinct taste;

not for everybody.

FASCINATING

you are fragile
yet resilient
like the heart that beats
despite
all its breaking.

how fascinating your heart is
for withstanding all the pain
you're
holding.

A THOUSAND SUNS

you are
worth more than a thousand suns
and i don't mean to be poetic but
you are
so full of worth
it's seeping out of your skin
it permeates the air
i breathe it
in

YOU PT. III

you can't be forecasted
you're not winter but you
have seasons;
unpredictable,
not a simple math equation;
skin & bones,
fragile &
resilient.

MADE OF LOVE

it's within
whenever you need it –
reach in.

reach deep
if you have to.

you have to know
it is everywhere you go –
you are never without it,
made from it.

MY BODY

a place i can
fully rest, feel welcome,
my best.

a place i feel free to be
myself;
a place like no where
else.

SELF-LOVE PT. II

there's a time and place for everything
but it's
always the right time
to love
myself

EMOTIONAL AVAILABILITY IS SUCH A VIBE

i grow when i go through the (e)motions –
it is not 'low vibe'
annoying or
inconvenient;
emotional availability is such a vibe

life is full of experiences that break our hearts:
death,
disappointments,
abuse,
divorce,
addiction,
failures,
loss

our spiritual strength
lies in being affected,
not in being above it

REVOLUTION

anger inspires progress –
through art, music, poetry.
an emotion that helps society
reflect and expand.

redirect your anger.
try your hand at something
creative.
i was never
a writer.
it was something
i picked up later.

tell the world what you
see. what requires our attention?
redirect your anger and
cause
a
revolution.

WHEN WE EMBRACE THEM

we don't fear our feelings,
we fear what happens
when we
embrace
them.

FEELING YOUR EMOTIONS

what if God said
it was supposed
to
hurt?

SADNESS

the reason i feel that sadness is gold is because it
embellishes
my growth. i used to find my depths so
uncomfortable, until i began to see my universe as a
beautifully written story – where both my grief and
happiness were the stars. i used to toy with questions
like "is depth a gift or a curse?" – but then i learned
that it's simply a path to even greater happiness. our
ocean of emotions cannot thrive without one or the
other – its glory comes from all evidence of life that
is below the surface.

HER CRIES

every day my spirit cried.
locked up, down below.
she has been through things
you'll never know.

the only way to soothe her cries
was to make them known.

ELEMENTS

you took up the task
of being somebody else's idea
of perfection, and
got used to shape-shifting to
meet somebody else's expectations.

you rejected
the parts of you they didn't
like.
but this hurt you more
than it built you up.

you won't conflate growth
with self-annihilation.
or diminish yourself in
the name of self-betterment.

you accept that you
are made of harmony and
contradictions –

a marriage of

elements.

ON ANGER

expressing anger
is not
the same
as
serving someone
your piece of
mind;
although sometimes
that's exactly what's
on the menu.

i express anger by
running;
through safely
smashing bottles in a
rage room.

anger fuels
revolutions
and progress;
it fuels
our cognizance of
right and
wrong;
it's our personal
alarm!

THERE'S NO SHAME

there's no shame in
feeling
a grief
so strong –
the strength of
which is proportional to
the love that
preceded it

EVEN SHADOWS NEED TO BE HUGGED

can you love your
darker parts?
hidden in the corner of your being –
punished for misbehaving.
hug them so tightly that they melt and turn into a
sweet nectar for your own
nourishment or
another's.

even shadows need to be hugged.

YOU'RE NOT TOO MUCH

what's right for you will not ask you to hide yourself.

your complexities. your passions.
the thoughts you have, your imaginations.

they're not too much
and you're not too complicated.

i know it's scary to be yourself,
and being rejected is not fun.

but the parts you hide from them
are the best
ones.

WE ARE THE THINGS WE LOVE FOR NO REASON

pay attention
to your
heart-centred nudges.
they may be loud
or quiet, obvious or subtle –
we are the things we love for no reason.

INNER-CHILD

the part of us who needs nurturing,
our presence.
the one who needs gentle
treatment.

children are helpless. they rely on us
adults to feed them, clothe them, protect them from
hurts –
physical, emotional,
spiritual.

the truth
of our upbringing reveals the truth of our
being.
it matters if we were loved –
if we were seen.
our experience
at this tender age
shapes our well-being.

persistent neglect or abuse
makes us prone to
addiction and depression.[8]
so are we

---

[8] The Effect of Multiple Adverse Childhood Experiences on Health:
A Systematic Review and Meta-Analysis (Hughes, Bellis, Hardcastle,
Sethi, Butchart, Mikton, Jones, Dunne 2017)

shit at life,
or are we living what's already
written?

will we thrive?
will we barely hold on?
will we feel safe in the world?
will we have healthy relationships?
we are not a statistic,
we are humans.
we are not a trendy topic,
this is our life.

i had the pleasure of meeting my inner-child.
she was five.
i cried.
i held her
until love equalled safety,
respect,
kindness.

that's the mission.
to reconnect with and
love the child
within us
and release their burdens.

GOD IS

reclaim authority over your faculties –
your emotions,
thoughts,
sensations.

pay attention –
the devil is
not
in the details,
God
is.

GOD'S HANDS

the love i have for myself stands on
a foundation built
by God's hands

THE GIVER

nothing is too
much
for the
One who
created everything
the size of
the gift
does not depend
on the recipient
it depends on who's
giving

A PRAYER:

to the One who responds to my cries,
please remove the
anxiety that is eating
at my
chest

ALREADY PERFECT

we are so busy perfecting ourselves,
we forget
we are already perfect
in His
eyes.

THE PERFECT ONE

my soul was perfected
by the One who makes no mistakes –
make no mistake.

BEING ALIVE BREAKS MY HEART

i am chosen by the
One
who mends my heart every time
the world breaks it

NEVER ABLE TO LAUGH

i have faith in
things unseen –
in my Creator,
in miracles.

if i don't, i'll never be able to
laugh.

YOU WILL FLY

He has knowledge of
every silent
cry your heart
has made;
He is the
all-compassionate.

you were made by His hands
and you will fly with
His wings.

CHOICES

criticism is bitter,
help is sweet,
if you had to choose,
don't make them weep.

MORE ABOUT LOVE

what it means to be loved:
- to be held
- to be supported
- to be accepted
- to be seen
- to be heard
- to be respected
- to be celebrated
- to be believed

love is a quiet force
that
reveals
our highest
form

LEAP INTO LOVE

why do you *fall* in love?
don't treat love like an accident!

leap into love –
with surrender
and
intent.

KINDNESS

kindness is not weak.
for it was only kindness that had the power
to shatter
my shield.

MY HAND IS YOURS

you
have the
strength to
bring
peace
to your soul

but if
you get tired
my hand
is yours
to hold

MORE TIMES THAN WE CAN REMEMBER

we might not have a certificate for these
accomplishments, but these are just as important:
- knowing something helpful that we didn't before
  - being good at something we weren't
- following through with something we didn't even
  want to start
  - taking care of our health as best we can

we have crossed multiple finish lines and
picked ourselves up more times
than we can even
remember.

SETTING BOUNDARIES

gently and firmly
gently and firmly
but more firmly
this time

REFLEX

maintaining
my peace
is as reflexive
as
breathing

FEAR IS MY FRIEND

maybe our dreams do not live on the other side of
fear,
but in it.

fear is really a friend
coaxing us to
take what is
in its
hand.

IN RETURN

if you ease my soul,
no doubt yours
will be eased
in
return

THE LOVE WE HAD

and when we're dead we'll
realise nothing mattered
but the love we had for
ourselves
and others

BIG ENOUGH

it was through loving you
with forgiveness and compassion
that my heart grew big
enough
to embrace the world

RELATIONSHIPS

take a moment to ask yourself
if you're mature;
if you are willing to have the difficult conversations;
if you're willing to accept that i can be difficult;
if you know who you are;
if your intentions are pure;
if you will treat me right;
if you'll be honest – every time –
i'll take a moment
to do the same.

A SOLID FOUNDATION PT. II

to
make love
last, be friends first.

ISMAIL

our meeting was predestined;
it was God's mercy.

i would not have
survived if He had
designed my life
differently.

you raised your status
in God's eyes
through piety
but the rewards were
reaped
by me.

ISMAIL (WISER THAN THAT)

i suffer from the memories we created –
our car rides to school in your *kelisa* and
your *kain pelikat*;
the months we would recite
the Quran together –
you said i impressed you with
my *tajwid*,
but really the impression
was made on me.

you spoke to me like an old friend –
"don't you have
anything better to
do than finish
all my food!" –
everyone knows i can't
take a joke,
but with you it was
different.

you got greyer, less mobile –
"all i do is stare at the wall.
if you can't visit me
it's enough if you called,"
i often recall you
saying.

i've not

said this
out loud, but while
preparing my life for
your departure, i forgot
you were still
alive.

i don't believe in regrets but
i wish i had been
wiser
than that.

TO BELONG AND TO BE LOVED

all we wish for
work for
ache for is to
belong
and to
be loved

ICE

etched in my memory
your love
the way
it reached
me
your eyes
the way they
saw me

my best friend
is it possible to
wish i had given
you
more
to thank you
for
your consistent presence
your love
you

thank yous and i love yous
will never be enough because i
never got enough
of
you

ON LOSS

we keep them alive
by building
them a home
in our hearts,
where we visit sometimes.

LEARN ME

learn what my soul needs.

the doors are open,
sit in.

the class size is small
but it works.

we'll go over the basics:
my boundaries and fears.

questions are welcome,
kindness matters.

IT CAN ALSO HURT

love,
don't hurt yourself proving your
worth.
they say pressure makes diamonds,
but it can also
hurt.

love,
there is no competition.
go at a comfortable pace.
your success looks different.

love,
ignore social expectations,
take it slow and steady,

enjoy your journey.

A BALANCED DIET

watch what you feed your mind,
heart, and soul.
notice what they digest easily
and what they reject.

COLOURS AND TEXTURES

perfection exists – it exists in our symmetry. we do
not work separately. together, we have all the colours
and textures we need to paint this mind-blowing,
mind-bending picture called life.

THE SUN

the sun
does not pretend
to be
the moon –
look at what happens
with a confidence
like
that.

it nourishes everything
it touches.

MAYBE THE UNITED NATIONS SHOULD...

maybe the united nations should change how they measure and
rank the well-being of countries. maybe it's not about policies
but whether their people can laugh despite their adversities.
if they sing and dance with their neighbours, not how hard they work.
if they are curious about the little things and the big things.

if their souls are as light as a feather.

TALKING TO MYSELF THROUGH MY ANXIETY

i've learned a million things to soothe my
anxieties
a million ways to find relief
i breathe amidst the chaos to find peace
i whisper *they won't kill you –*
these feelings underneath
your
skin

OVERCOMER

it doesn't matter how small you feel, how beaten
down you've been, or how tired you are from fighting
your demons alone. what matters is that you keep
your self-belief intact, build your foundations, and
seek help. you are not here by accident, you are here
by design – within that design is the blueprint to your
success. so, take a deep breath and trust that you will
overcome this test.

FORGIVE YOURSELF

when you're healing from a relationship, the first person who deserves your forgiveness is yourself. forgive yourself for allowing chaos into your life. forgive yourself for not having boundaries. forgive yourself for ignoring the warning signs. forgive yourself for being stupid (lol).

some things i learned about love from my most loyal
companion Ice (i spent half my life with her; she
passed away in 2020 from kidney failure):
- relationships might be temporary but the love
you cultivated is permanent
- love feels special, intentional, and expansive
- to love and be loved hurts but it is through
loving and being loved that our greatest potential
is realised
- caring for our loved ones in sickness is never in
vain. they will meet God and tell Him *protect them
because they protected me. love them because they loved
me. nurture them because they nurtured me. provide for
them because they provided for me.*

WHY I RUN #13

i am no athlete by any definition and running hurts my feet but on days when i can muster it, i run to feel my most powerful. no one has ever told me that running would make me feel strong and fearless. no one has ever told me that running would make me feel more like

me.

LOVED

they say you don't know
what you got until it's gone
but finally getting
what you never received
hit different too

MY HAPPINESS DON'T COST A THING

i don't know if money can buy
happiness
but i know the
happiest people in the
world
are not happy because of it

i don't know if money can buy
happiness
but i know the
unhappiest people in the
world
have it

i don't know if money can buy happiness but i'd
rather my happiness not cost a thing.

CONFLICTS AND VICTORIES

how meaningless our stories would be
if we knew what to expect
conflicts would feel boring
and victories would feel less exciting
if we all knew what came next

THE LANGUAGE OF MY HEART

you may not speak my language
too old or lazy to learn it
but understanding what my heart means when it is
speaking
is worth the commitment

AFFIRMATION #1

only good things will come
to
me from now on
i've let go
of the things that weigh a
tonne
i deserve it much i deserve it
now i deserve what
i need and
want

SELF-BELIEF

some people live with chronic pain
i live with chronic stress
i can't feel the freedom of success without
the weight of my
tests

they call it life but i call it a
trauma response when all i've done is
find ways to keep from losing
my mind
cultivating peace has been the toughest
mountain to climb
but i find the views
up there worth my
time

to get there nothing works as well as my
breath
to get there nothing works but faith in
myself

AT WAR

be gentle, my darling
i know it's hard to do
so beautiful and magnificent yet
at war with who you've turned
into
longing for acceptance
longing to belong
longing to be loved for exactly who
you've become (your real self)

SELF-LOVE PT. III

they think it's weird that i love
myself they think it's conceited
they think it's weird that i
nurture myself gently when i'm wounded
they think i'm weird for adoring my strengths
that i admire who i am
but if it's normal to love, adore, and admire
others
it is normal to love
myself

I SMILE AS I WRITE THIS

the pain has subsided
the anger vanished
as i stop looking at the past with animosity but
forgiveness
i smile as i write this
my mind at ease
my heart rejoicing at its newfound
peace

THE HEART REMEMBERS

we are taught to forgive
for forgiveness' sake
it frees us up, they say
but the heart remembers
so does it really free us?
someone once told me
it is okay if you can't forgive
can you accept that too?
that took me by surprise
because isn't the mature thing to do to
forgive, forget, and move on?
it took me years but i found my
answers
when i forgive i am letting you off the hook
it is an act of compassion
it is a favour of sorts
it is a gift – the best
ones come from the
heart
it is okay if i cannot forgive
one day i will but today i will welcome my feelings
about it

A BLANK CANVAS

we toil and labour to turn our dreams into reality but
sometimes no matter what we do nothing changes.
these roadblocks are simply an invitation to switch
paths. it is an invitation to close a chapter and move
towards something more fulfilling – and sometimes
that means moving away from things that don't fulfil
us anymore. new projects or experiences that fill our
hearts with passion and love are always available to
us. i've learned that i am not obligated to stick to a
vision or idea that doesn't want to be mine. i am
welcome to reinvent myself when it is time.
sometimes the blank canvas intimidates us – but life
always finds a way to work itself out (and i like to
think i'm stronger than my fears).

TRUE PARTNERSHIP

being in a relationship was where i found
comfort but no matter what i did i never found
true partnership
i learned to find comfort in my
aloneness, and began
to grow
filling that empty space with my passions and
interests
the empty space being my heart not my
environment
being in a relationship with others is great but being
in a relationship with myself takes the cake

TAMAT (THE END)

I don't suppose you've realised that there are more Loves than Not-loves. The ways to interpret this are thus one, there are more things that enrich the heart than there are things that break it; two, it does not take much to break a heart and a lot to mend it.

ABOUT THE AUTHOR

Yasmin's heart is most content when she is creating content from the heart. She discovered her passion for words while studying a course entitled "Reflective and Creative Practices for Social Change" at the Institute of Development Studies based at the University of Sussex.

She is the creator of **Pause** and the host of the Pause with Yasmin podcast.

She grew up in Kuala Lumpur, Malaysia.

@yasminjasmy | @pauseuniverse | www.mind-pause.com

Made in the USA
Monee, IL
07 July 2026

56549921R00125